Athletes Who Made a Difference

MEGAN RAPINOE

Josh Anderson

illustrated by Casey Ella Fredrick

Graphic Universe™ • Minneapolis

Graphic Universe™
An imprint of Lerner Publishing Group, Inc.
241 First Avenue North
Minneapolis, MN 55401 USA

For reading levels and more information, look up this title at www.lernerbooks.com.

Main body text set in CCDaveGibbonsLower
Typeface provided by Comicraft

Photo Acknowledgments
The images in this book are used with the permission of: © Steph Chambers/Staff/Getty Images, p. 28 (left); © Robin Alam/ISI Photos/USSF/Contributor/Getty Images, p. 28 (right).

Library of Congress Cataloging-in-Publication Data

Names: Anderson, Josh, author. I Fredrick, Casey Ella, illustrator.
Title: Megan Rapinoe : athletes who made a difference / Josh Anderson ; [illustrated by Casey Ella Fredrick].
Description: Minneapolis, MN : Graphic Universe, [2024] I Series: Athletes who made a difference I Includes bibliographical references and index. I Audience: Ages 8–12 years I Audience: Grades 4–6 I Summary: "This graphic biography shows how Megan Rapinoe's accomplishments on and off the soccer field have made her a household name. Read all about her many wins, from Olympic gold to the Presidential Medal of Freedom"— Provided by publisher.
Identifiers: LCCN 2023049765 (print) I LCCN 2023049766 (ebook) I ISBN 9781728492971 (library binding) I ISBN 9798765628010 (paperback) I ISBN 9798765631232 (epub)
Subjects: LCSH: Rapinoe, Megan, 1985-—Juvenile literature. I Women soccer players—United States—Biography—Juvenile literature. I Lesbian soccer players—United States—Biography—Juvenile literature. I Women Olympic athletes—United States—Biography—Juvenile literature. I Political activists—United States—Biography—Juvenile literature. I Equal pay for equal work—Juvenile literature. I Presidential Medal of Freedom—Juvenile literature.
Classification: LCC GV942.7.R366 A53 2024 (print) I LCC GV942.7.R366 (ebook) I DDC 796.334092 [B]—dc23/eng/20231213

LC record available at https://lccn.loc.gov/2023049765
LC ebook record available at https://lccn.loc.gov/2023049766

Manufactured in the United States of America
1 – CG – 7/15/24

Table of Contents

CHAPTER 1
ELITE JUNIOR

Megan Rapinoe was born on July 5, 1985, in Redding, California. Megan is a twin. She and her sister Rachael were the youngest children in a big family. They had five other siblings and stepsiblings.

Megan and Rachael idolized their brother Brian. They followed him everywhere.

Wait for us!

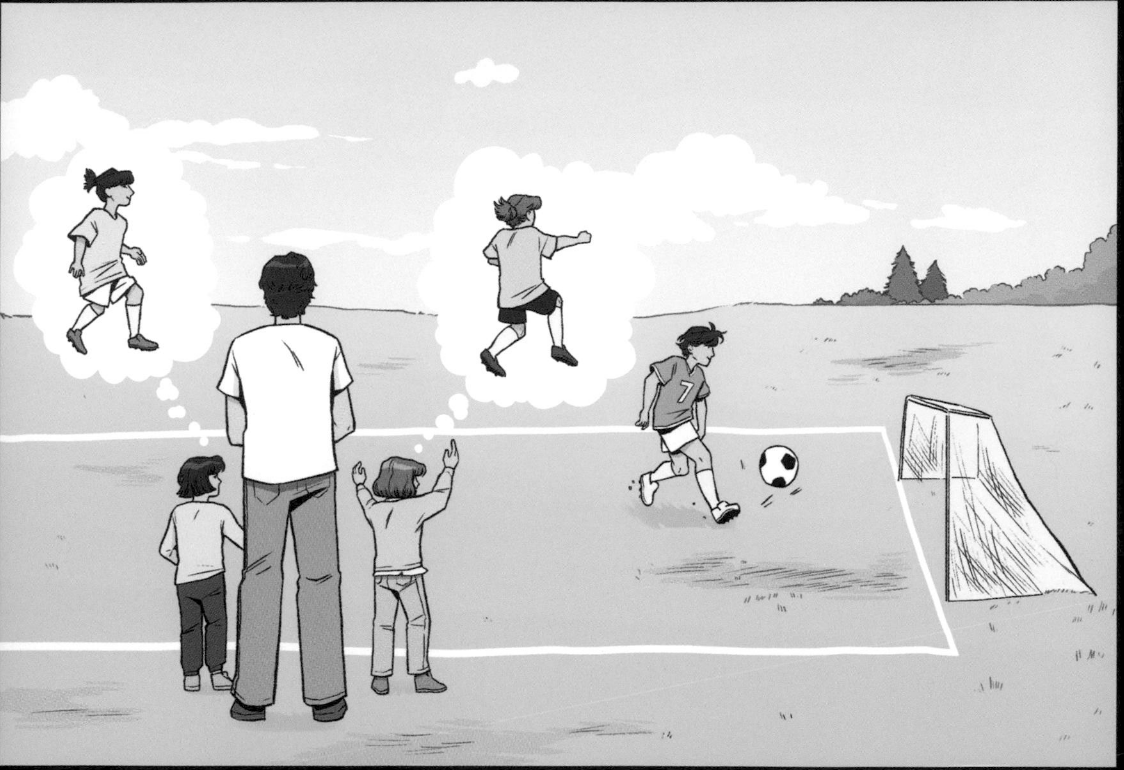

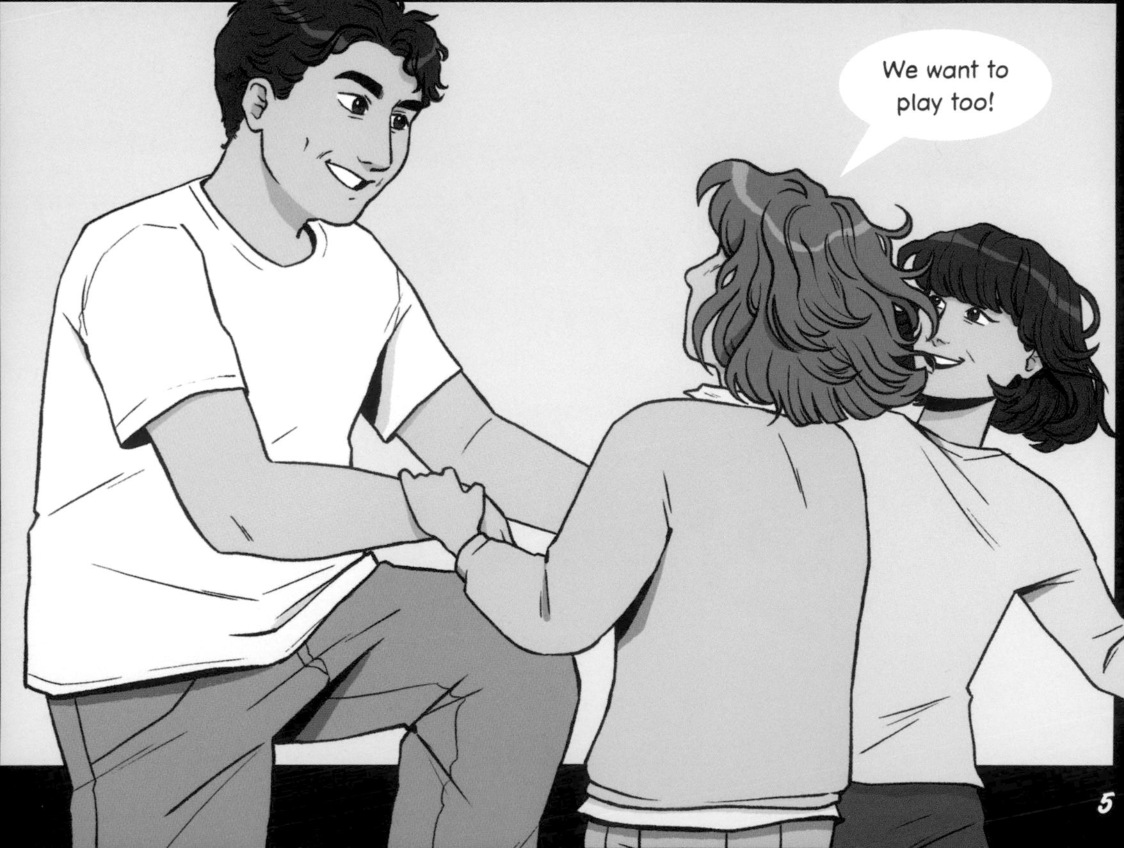
We want to play too!

Both Rapinoe sisters proved to be strong athletes. In addition to soccer, they would go on to run track and play basketball in high school.

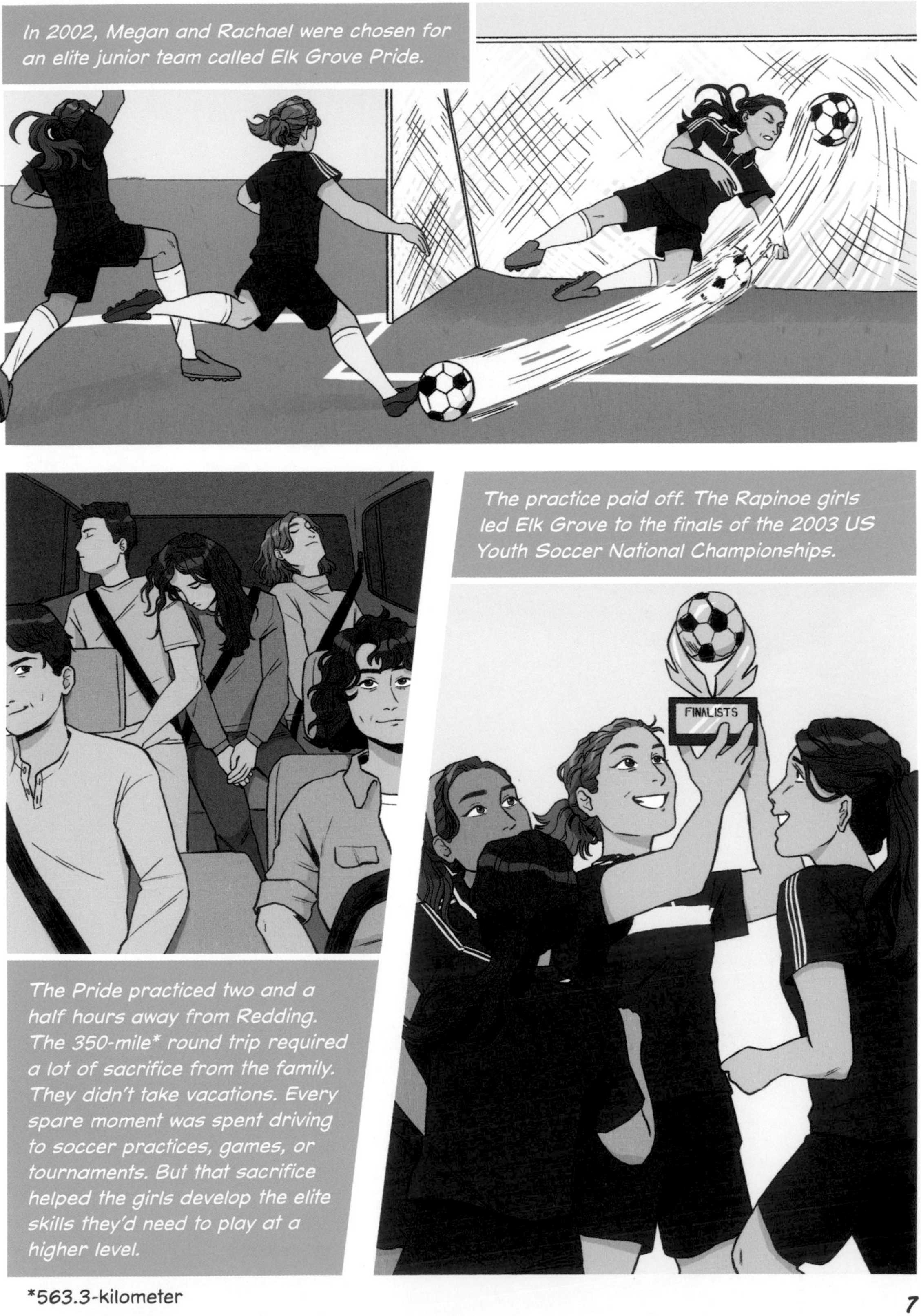
In 2002, Megan and Rachael were chosen for an elite junior team called Elk Grove Pride.
The Pride practiced two and a half hours away from Redding. The 350-mile* round trip required a lot of sacrifice from the family. They didn't take vacations. Every spare moment was spent driving to soccer practices, games, or tournaments. But that sacrifice helped the girls develop the elite skills they'd need to play at a higher level.
The practice paid off. The Rapinoe girls led Elk Grove to the finals of the 2003 US Youth Soccer National Championships.
FINALISTS

*563.3-kilometer

CHAPTER 2

THE PATH FORWARD

Megan was chosen to represent the United States at the 2004 FIFA Under-19 Women's World Championship. That year, the competition took place in Thailand.

Megan scored three goals in the tournament. She helped the US finish third.

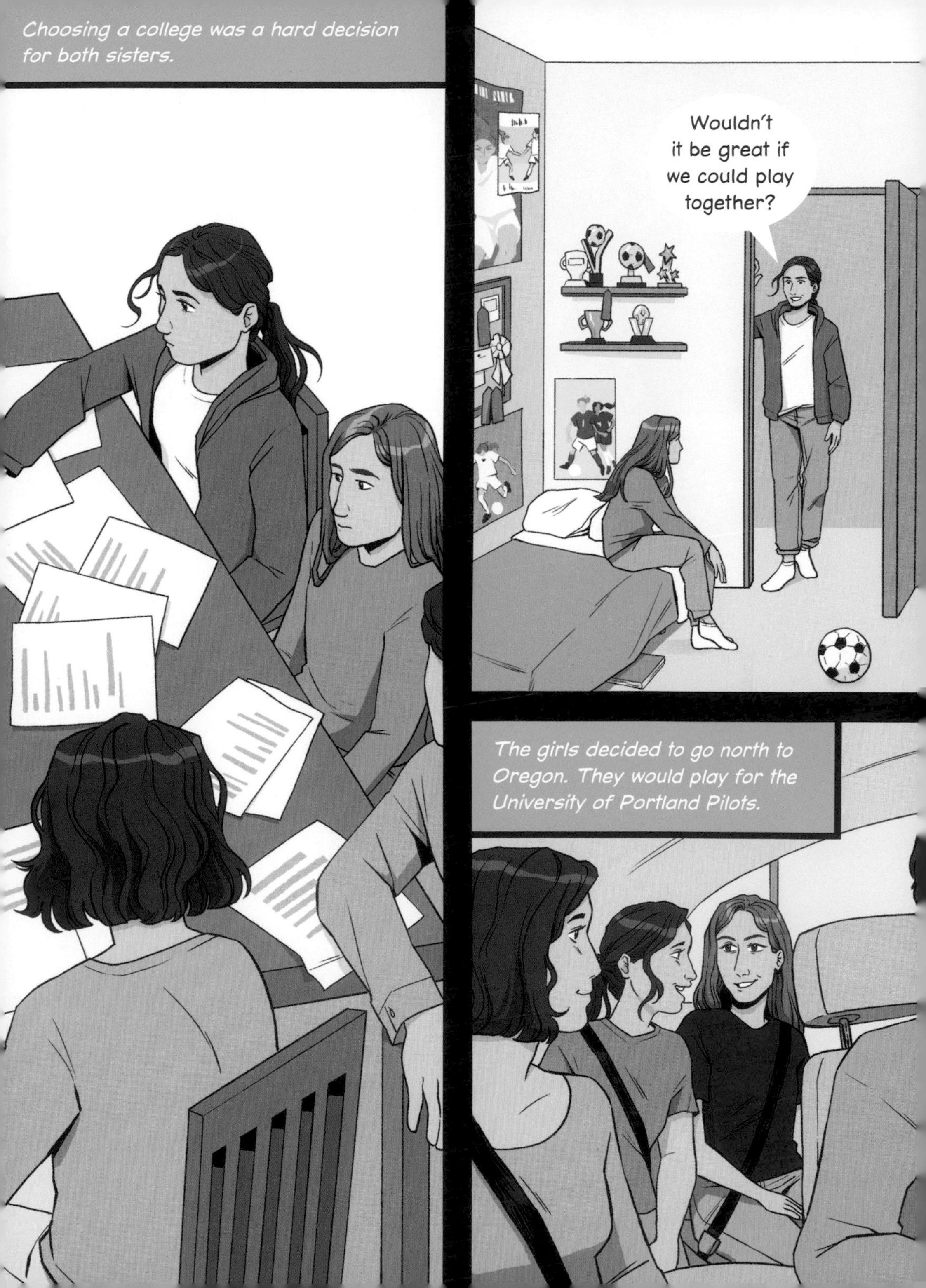
Choosing a college was a hard decision for both sisters.
Wouldn't it be great if we could play together?
The girls decided to go north to Oregon. They would play for the University of Portland Pilots.

With Megan playing, the Portland Pilots went undefeated in 2005.

She scored seven game-winning goals that season. The University of Portland won the NCAA Women's Soccer Championship.

Yes! Of course I'm available.

After her excellent freshman season, Megan received a call she'd been waiting for her entire life.

Megan was invited to play for the US Women's Senior National Team. The team represents the United States at the FIFA Women's World Cup and the Summer Olympic Games.

In October 2006, the United States faced off against Chinese Taipei in the Women's World Cup. There, Megan scored her first two goals for the US National Team. But then . . .

Less than a week later, Megan was back on the field with the University of Portland. On October 5, she suffered a season-ending injury to her anterior cruciate ligament (ACL).

Megan worked hard to come back from her injury. It was a long, slow process.

Only two games into the 2007 season, Megan reinjured the same knee.

Not again!

The injuries kept her sidelined for nearly two years. She made herself a promise. When she finally made it back onto the pitch, she would make sure to truly appreciate playing the game.

CHAPTER 3
FINDING A VOICE

In 2009, Megan began dating Australian soccer player Sarah Walsh.

Their friends and families knew they were together. But Megan and Sarah decided not to share news of their dating with the public. Many people in the US still did not accept LGBTQIA+ relationships.

The Defense of Marriage Act (DOMA) had been US law since 1996. It said that the US federal government would not recognize same-sex marriages.

As an added barrier, some states actually banned same-sex marriage.

But by the early 2000s, LGBTQIA+ rights were getting more and more support. It was time to provide equality to all.

Megan was named to the US roster for the 2011 FIFA Women's World Cup in Germany.

Late in a quarterfinal match with Brazil, Team USA trailed its opponent by one goal. They were about to be eliminated from the World Cup.

We're into the 122nd minute of play here. Time is about to run out for Team USA.

Here goes nothing.

I can't believe it! Rapinoe sent in a perfect cross, and Wambach headed it in!

The game came down to penalty kicks, and Team USA made it out on top. They advanced to the finals, where they lost to Japan.

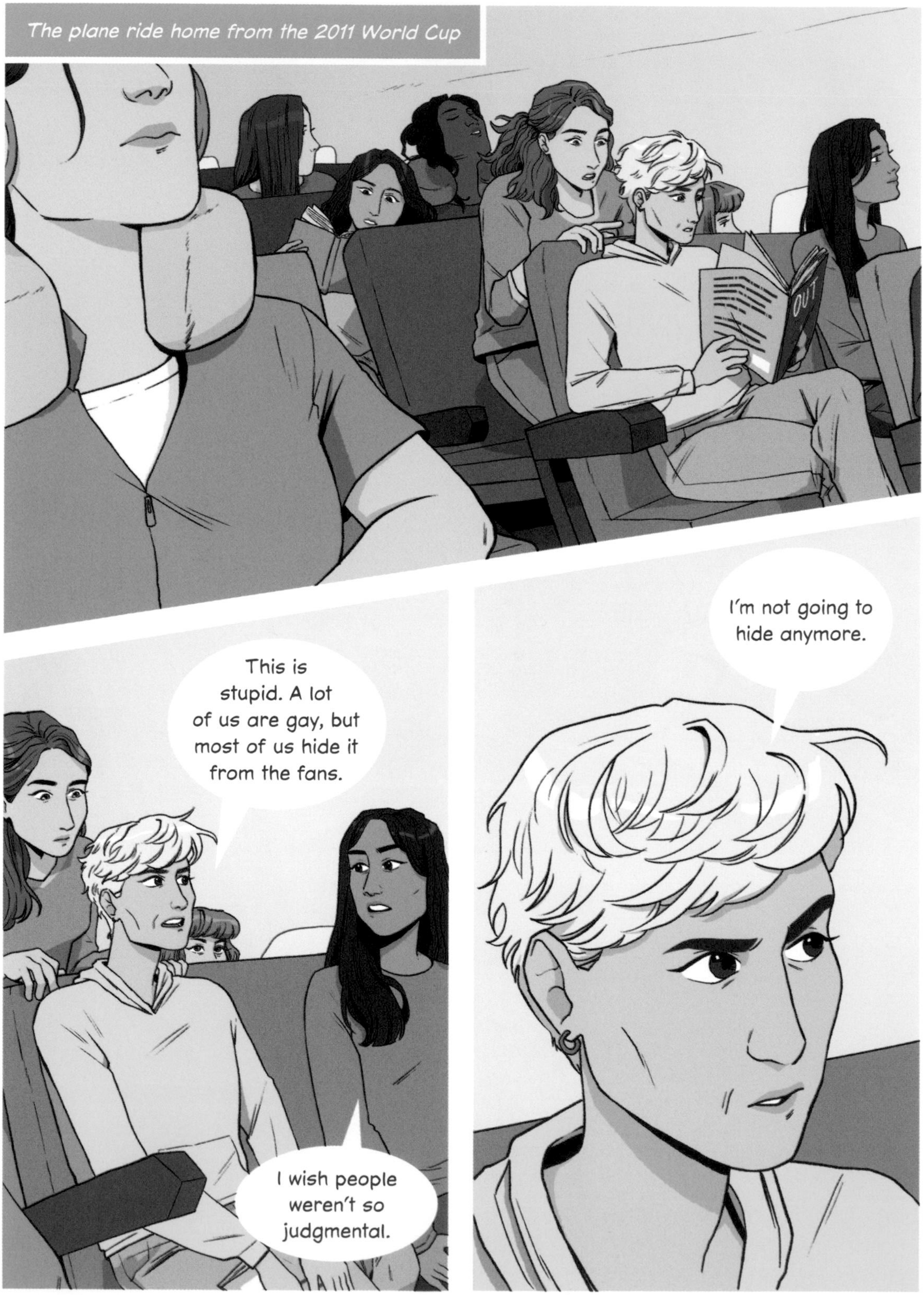
The plane ride home from the 2011 World Cup
OUT
This is stupid. A lot of us are gay, but most of us hide it from the fans.
I wish people weren't so judgmental.
I'm not going to hide anymore.

Sports in general are still homophobic, in the sense that not a lot of people are out.

When Megan returned home, she scheduled an interview with Out *magazine*. It was time to tell the world she was gay.

People want—they *need*—to see that there are people like me playing *soccer* for the good ol' U.S. of A.

Coming out refers to letting someone else know your sexual orientation or gender identity. It can be a difficult, emotional process. Megan hoped that coming out would set a positive example for others.

On June 26, 2015, the US Women's National Team defeated China in a quarterfinal match at the FIFA Women's World Cup.

That same day, the US Supreme Court ruled on Obergefell v. Hodges. This case granted same-sex couples the same rights as opposite-sex couples in all 50 states. That includes the right to marry.

There were victories on and off the field. The US went on to win the 2015 World Cup.

After scoring two goals in the tournament, Megan was selected to the World Cup All-Star Team.

	US Women's National team (since 1991)	US Men's National team (since 1930)
World Cup Championship	4	0
Olympic Gold Medals	4	0

Despite a much more successful record and their 2015 World Cup win, players on the US Women's Team were paid significantly less than the US Men's Team. Their stadiums and non-tournament pay was inferior too.

And we win more! So let's do something about it!

Megan and four of her teammates filed a complaint with the Equal Employment Opportunity Commission (EEOC). The EEOC is part of the US government. It makes sure laws about anti-discrimination are followed. The complaint pointed out the difference in pay between the men's and women's teams.

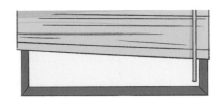

Megan and her teammates are not alone. In 2022, women in the United States earned 17 percent less than men for doing the same jobs. This is called the wage gap.

Even as the fight for equal pay continued, Megan dominated her competition on the field. Team USA swept the 2019 FIFA Women's World Cup.

At the same time, thousands of fans chanted for equality.

Equal pay!
Equal pay!
Equal pay!

Megan scored six goals in the tournament. She was given the Golden Boot award for this accomplishment.

She was also awarded the Golden Ball award. It goes to the World Cup's best player.

We have nothing more to prove. The time for equal pay is now!

Success on the pitch wasn't going to stop Megan. She was never going to stop fighting for what she felt was right.

Megan went to Washington, DC. She spoke to Congress and at the White House. She spoke passionately for equal pay and rights for transgender people.

I've been devalued, disrespected, and dismissed because I'm a woman. . . . Despite all the wins, I'm still paid less than men who do the same job that I do.

In 2022, the US Soccer Federation agreed to provide equal pay for the Women's and Men's National Soccer Teams. Seven years after Megan and her teammates first spoke up, women's soccer finally received what it had been fighting for.

In 2023, Megan announced she would play in her last World Cup. But her impact on the National Team will be felt long after she hangs up her cleats for good.

AFTERWORD

Megan started playing with the Seattle-based team OL Reign in 2013. They are part of the National Women's Soccer League (NWSL). She suited up for the US Women's National Team in the 2023 FIFA Women's World Cup. At 37 years old, she was one of the older players on the team. She also felt the pressure of leading the team to another victory. Her main message to her younger teammates? Just focus on the game.

Megan is engaged to her partner, basketball star Sue Bird. In 2022, they launched a production company together called A Touch More. They want to tell the stories of "revolutionaries who move the culture forward." Both Megan and Sue know they have a responsibility as professional athletes to make a difference in the world.

In 2022, Megan gave an impassioned speech after the US Supreme Court overturned Roe v. Wade. This ruling took away a woman's right to choose what to do with her own body. Megan has also become a major voice defending the rights of trans athletes to compete in women's sports. Encouraging inclusion and making it easier for any and all athletes to play will only help competition.

In July 2023, Megan announced that she was going to retire at the end of the season. Her fourth World Cup would be her last. In September, she played two friendly games in Chicago against South Africa. They were her final international matches with the National Women's Soccer League. Her last professional regular season game was on October 15.

ATHLETE SNAPSHOT

BIRTH NAME: Megan Anna Rapinoe

NICKNAME: Pinoe

BORN: July 5, 1985

Awards of Note

- ◆ 2012, 2016, 2020—three-time Olympian, two-time Olympic medalist

- ◆ 2019—*Sports Illustrated* Sportsperson of the Year

- ◆ 2019—Best FIFA Women's Player

- ◆ 2020—*TIME* magazine's 100 Most Influential People

- ◆ 2022—Presidential Medal of Freedom

SOURCE NOTES

19   Matt Brooks, "U.S. Soccer Star Megan Rapinoe: 'For the Record: I am *Gay*,'" *Washington Post*, July 3, 2012, https://www.washingtonpost.com/blogs/early-lead/post /us-soccer-star-megan-rapinoe-for-the-record-i-am -gay/2012/07/03/gJQAuq27KW_blog.html

19   Charlie Brinkhurst-Cuff, "In Praise of the Mighty Megan Rapinoe: 'I Felt Her Defiance and I Revelled In It," *The Guardian*, July 1, 2019, https://www.theguardian.com /football/shortcuts/2019/jul/01/in-praise-of-the-mighty -megan-rapinoe-i-felt-her-defiance-and-i-revelled-in-it

26   Sarah Ewall-Wice, Kathryn Watson, "Megan Rapinoe Visits White House with Women's Soccer Team on Equal Pay Day," *CBS News*, March 24, 2021, https://www.cbsnews.com/news /megan-rapinoe-equal-pay-day-hearing-watch-live-stream-to day-2021-03-24/

GLOSSARY

act: a law, or proposed law, passed by Congress

anterior cruciate ligament: one of the key ligaments that helps stabilize the knee; also called the ACL

anti-discrimination: a law designed to prevent discrimination against a group of people

championship: a series of games or matches designed to decide a single winner

cross: a pass to the area in front of the goal in an attempt to score

elite: at the highest level

homophobic: showing prejudice against members of the LGBTQIA+ community

LGBTQIA+: an abbreviation used to represent people in the lesbian, gay, bisexual, trans, queer or questioning, intersex, asexual, and more community

penalty kick: a free kick at the goal awarded to a team after a foul by their opponent

roster: a list of active players

sidelined: unable to play for a team or in a game

FURTHER INFORMATION

Blumenthal, Karen. *Let Me Play: The Story of Title IX: The Law That Changed the Future of Girls in America.* New York: Atheneum Books for Young Readers, 2022.

Olympics: Soccer
https://www.nbcolympics.com/soccer

Portland Pilots: Megan Rapinoe
https://portlandpilots.com/sports/womens-soccer/roster/megan
-rapinoe/1358

Rapinoe, Megan. *One Life: Adapted for Young Readers.* New York: Razorbill, 2021.

Schwartz, Heather E. *US Women's National Soccer Team: Winning On and Off the Field.* Minneapolis: Lerner Publications, 2024.

Team USA: Megan Rapinoe
https://www.teamusa.org/us-soccer/athletes/megan-rapinoe

US Women's National Team
https://www.ussoccer.com/teams/uswnt

INDEX